PORTUGUESE

Colophon

© 2004 Rebo International b.v., Lisse, The Netherlands

www.rebo-publishers.com – info@rebo-publishers.com

Original recipes and photographs: © R&R Publishing Pty. Ltd.

Design, editing and production: AMOS Typographic Studio, Prague, The Czech Republic

Cover design: Minkowsky Graphics, Enkhuizen, The Netherlands

ISBN 90 366 1627 1

PORTUGUESE

sweet melancholy from the fado restaurant for

creative cooking

REBO
PUBLISHERS

Foreword

Portugal is a culinary paradise.

It is also a country of famous sailors and intrepid travelers, dreamy towns sleeping in between centuries old olive groves, moot castles, gothic cathedrals and superb coastal plains. But above all, it is a culinary paradise. What other country can offer such lovely dishes as Sardinas grelhadas, grilled sardines, and Bacalhau, the famous angelfish for which there are 365 methods of preparation?

In this cookbook, you will be introduced to the authentic Portuguese kitchen. Naturally, there are many delightful fish dishes, but also original soups, such as Sopa de pedra, Stone soup. According to legend, Stone Soup was made from water and stones by a clever monk beggar. The Portuguese also make delicious sweet deserts, such as baked almonds and Figos com porto, figs with – you guessed it! – port. You only need nice melancholy fado music to complete the atmosphere of a Portuguese restaurant.

Contents

portuguese

Cut figs in half. **Wrap** a piece of prosciutto around each fig half.

Place the figs on a serving platter. **Drizzle** with extra virgin olive oil and red wine vinegar. Season with ground black pepper.

Figs with Proscuitto – Figos com Presunto

Ingredients

8 medium figs

16 slices prosciutto

2 tablespoons extra virgin olive oil

2 tablespoons red wine vinegar

Freshly ground black pepper

Heat 1 tablespoons oil in a frying pan over medium to high heat. Sear fish quickly, but do not cook fish through. **Remove** fish and place in a ceramic dish.

Heat remaining oil over medium heat, add garlic and cook for 30 seconds. Remove from heat. Combine oil with lemon juice and white wine vinegar.

Pour mixture over fish and add lemon slices, onions. parsley and coriander. Season with salt and pepper

Cover with plastic wrap and place in the fridge for 1-2 hours. Remove fish from marinade and cut into thin slices. **Arrange** on a serving plate with onions, lemon slices and herbs. Pour marinade over all.

Marinated Fish — Escabeche de Atum

Ingredients

5 tablespoons olive oil	1 lemon, halved and sliced
1lb/500g boneless tuna steaks	1 small red onions (Spanish), finely sliced
2 cloves garlic, crushed	2 tablespoons freshly chopped continental parsley
1/4 cup/60ml lemon juice	2 tablespoons freshly chopped coriander
2 tablespoons white wine vinegar	sea salt and freshly ground black pepper

Place cod in a saucepan of cold water. Bring to the boil and simmer for 30 minutes or until tender. Drain and rinse under cold water, leave to cool. **Remove** skin and bones and place in a food processor. Process until finely shredded.

Meanwhile place potatoes in a saucepan of water. Bring to the boil and simmer until potatoes are tender. **Drain** potatoes.

Place potatoes in a large bowl and mash until smooth. Add fish, flour, parsley, egg yolk and pepper. **Mix** together until smooth.

Beat egg white until stiff. Gently fold into the mixture.

Using two spoons shape mixture into oval fritters.

Heat enough oil in a frying pan to cook batches of fritters until light golden in color. Drain on paper towel.

Serve with lemon or lime wedges and piri piri sauce.

Salt Cod Fritters – Bolinchos de Bacalbau

Ingredients

1/2lb/250g boneless dried salt cod, soaked

*(see below)

1lb/500g potatoes, peeled and diced

1 tablespoon flour

2 tablespoons freshly chopped continental parsley

1 egg, separated

freshly ground black pepper

oil for cooking

lemon or lime wedges to serve

* Soak cod in a bowl of cold water. Cover with plastic wrap and place in the fridge for 24 hours, changing water 4 or 5 times. Drain cod, rinse well under cold water and drain again.

Preheat oven to 392°F/200 C. **Cut** the top from the garlic and wrap in aluminium foil. Place on a baking tray and bake for 40-45 minutes or until garlic is soft. When garlic is cool squeeze the garlic from the skin.

Place olives in a food processor with garlic, olive oil, lemon juice and pepper. Process until mixture is smooth.

Remove mixture from food processor and place in a small bowl, cover with plastic and place in the fridge.

Serve with toasted wood-fired bread or crackers.

Olive Tapenade –
Pasta de Azeitonas Pretas

Ingredients

1 head garlic

1 cup/300g pitted black olives

1 tablespoon extra virgin olive oil

2 tablespoons lemon juice

freshly ground black pepper

Blanch asparagus in a saucepan of boiling water for 2 minutes. Drain and refresh under cold water. Pat dry with paper towel and cut into three pieces.

Place egg in a mixing bowl and whisk until frothy. **Add** flour, baking powder, salt and water. Whisk together until light and smooth.

Heat enough oil in a large frying pan. Dip asparagus in batter and cook in oil for 1-2 minutes or until golden. **Remove** with a slotted spoon and drain on paper towel. Season asparagus with salt and pepper and serve with lemon wedges.

Asparagus Fritters – Esparagos Fritos

Ingredients

2 bunches asparagus, trimmed
and cut into 2 or 3 pieces

1 egg

1 cup/200g plain flour

1 teaspoon baking powder

1/2 teaspoon salt

3/4-1 cup/175-250ml ice-cold water

oil for cooking

salt and freshly ground black pepper

lemon wedges to serve

Cook fava or broad beans in a saucepan of boiling water for 1 minute. Drain and rinse under cold water. Remove skins from the beans.

Place prosciutto on a baking tray and place under a hot grill. **Cook** for 1-2 minutes each side or until crisp. When cool, break into pieces.

Place broad beans, prosciutto and onion in a serving bowl. **Drizzle** extra virgin olive oil and white wine vinegar over mixture. Sprinkle with sugar, coriander and parsley and season with salt and pepper. **Toss** well to combine.

Broad Beans with Coriander –
Favos com Coentro

Ingredients

3 cups/690g shelled broad beans or fava beans

8 slices prosciutto   1/2 teaspoon sugar

1 small red onion (spanish) thinly sliced   2 tablespoons freshly chopped coriander (cilantro)

2 tablespoons extra virgin olive oil   1 tablespoon freshly chopped continental parsley

1 tablespoon white wine vinegar   salt and freshly ground black pepper

vegetables and salads

Cook beans in a saucepan of boiling water for 2-3 minutes or until they turn bright green. Drain and rinse under cold water.

Heat extra virgin olive oil in a frying pan over medium heat. **Add** garlic and tomatoes and cook for 3-4 minutes or until tomatoes are a little soft.

Add red wine vinegar, lemon juice, sugar and coriander. **Bring** to a boil. Remove from heat.

Place beans in a serving bowl. **Pour** tomato mixture over. Season with salt and pepper and toss to combine.

Green Beans and Tomatoes with Coriander and Garlic – Feijao Verde e Tomate com Coentro e Alho

Ingredients

1 1/2 cups/350g green beans, trimmed and halved

1/4 cup/60ml extra virgin olive oil

2 cloves garlic, crushed

1 cup/250g cherry tomatoes, halved

1 tablespoon red wine vinegar

1 tablespoon lemon juice

1/2 teaspoon sugar

1/4 cup/58g freshly chopped coriander (cilantro)

salt and freshly ground black pepper

vegetables and salads

Preheat oven to 428°F/220° C. Lightly grease a shallow casserole dish.

Heat vegetable stock in a large frying pan over medium heat. Add potato slices and cook for 8-10 minutes or until tender. **Drain** potatoes, saving 1/2 cup/118 ml, and rinse under cold water.

Cut red pepper into thin slices.

Arrange potato slices and red pepper in the casserole dish. Pour over stock. Arrange tomato slices on top. **Drizzle** with lemon juice and olive oil. Sprinkle with sugar and season with pepper.

Bake in the oven for 20 minutes or until tomatoes are cooked.

Garnish with parsley and coriander.

Potato and Tomato Pie — Bola de batata e tomate

Ingredients

3 cups/710ml vegetable stock

1 3/4lb/750g potatoes, peeled and thinly sliced

1 red pepper (capsicum), roasted *(see below)

2 tablespoons lemon juice

2 tablespoons olive oil

1/4 teaspoon sugar

freshly ground black pepper

1 tablespoon freshly chopped continental parsley

1 tablespoon freshly chopped coriander (cilantro)

5-6 roma tomatoes, sliced

* *To roast peppers* – cut pepper into four and remove seeds. Place on a baking tray and bake under a hot grill for 6-8 minutes or until skin blisters. Leave to cool then remove skin.

Preheat oven to 392°F/200 °C. Lightly grease a shallow casserole dish.

Heat olive oil in a frying pan over medium heat. Add onions, garlic and bacon and cook until golden. **Remove** and set aside.

Layer potatoes, onions, garlic and bacon in the casserole dish.

Mix together chicken stock, coriander, salt and pepper. **Pour** over the potatoes.

Bake in the oven for approximately 1 hour, or until cooked and golden on top. **Cover** with foil if the top starts to burn.

Ingredients

2 tablespoons olive oil

2 onions, sliced

2 cloves garlic, crushed

1 cup/200g smoked bacon or speck, diced

Potatoes with Bacon and Onion – Batatas à Moda do Alentejana

2.2lb/1kg potatoes (about 4), peeled and thinly sliced

1 cup/250ml chicken stock

1 tablespoons freshly chopped coriander (cilantro)

salt and freshly ground black pepper

Heat olive oil in a large frying pan over medium heat. Add sausage and cook for 2 minutes or until golden and crisp. Remove and set aside. **Add** onion, garlic, pepper and peas and cook until pepper and peas are tender.

Remove from heat. **Stir** through sausage, mint, parsley, salt and pepper.

Serve peas with poached eggs.

Ingredients

1 tablespoon olive oil

1 piece chourico or chorizo sausage,

thinly sliced

1 onion, finely chopped

2 cloves garlic, crushed

1 red pepper (capsicum),

deseeded and diced

1 yellow pepper (capsicum),

deseeded and diced

2 cups/500g fresh shelled peas

or frozen peas, thawed

1 tablespoon freshly chopped mint

1 tablespoon freshly chopped

continental parsley

salt and freshly ground black pepper

4 eggs, poached *(see below)

Peas with Chourico –
Ervilhas à Algarvia

* To poach eggs – Heat enough water and
1 tablespoon vinegar in a frying pan. Bring water
to simmering point. Break eggs into a cup and
gently slide into the water. Poach until just cooked.

Place red pepper on a baking tray and place under a hot grill for 6-8 minutes or until skin is blistered and black. Leave to cool. Remove skin and thinly slice.

Preheat oven to 350°F/180 °C. Place tomatoes on a baking tray lined with baking paper. Lightly spray or brush with olive oil and season with salt and pepper. Bake in the oven for 15-20 minutes or until just soft. Set aside.

Combine peppers, tomatoes, cucumber, red onion, olives, salad leaves and coriander in a large serving bowl.

Combine ingredients for dressing in a small jug. Pour dressing over salad and toss to combine.

Ingredients

1 red pepper (capsicum), deseeded and cut into quarters

3 vine ripened tomatoes, cut into wedges

1 tablespoon olive oil

1 small cucumber, sliced

1 small red onion (spanish), finely chopped

1/2 cup/115g black olives

1/2 cup/150g mixed green leaves (curly endive, baby spinach, butter lettuce and watercress)

1/4 cup/57g fresh coriander (cilantro) leaves

Mixed Salad – Salada à Portuguesa

Dressing

1/4 cup/60ml olive oil

1 tablespoon lemon juice

1 tablespoon red wine vinegar

1/2 teaspoon sugar

salt and freshly ground pepper

Heat oil in a large saucepan over medium heat. Cook onion and garlic until soft.

Add bacon and cook for 2 minutes. Add bacon bones, potatoes, carrots, turnips, celery, bay leaves and stock. **Bring** to a boil, reduce heat to low and simmer covered for 40-45 minutes or until vegetables are tender. If time permits, simmer for 1 hour. This gives the soup more flavor.

Add cabbage and kidney beans and simmer for a further 5 minutes. **Remove** ham hock or bacon bones and cut the meat into small pieces. Return meat to the saucepan, add parsley and season with salt and pepper.

Serve soup with crusty bread.

Ingredients

1 tablespoon olive oil

1 onion, finely chopped

2 cloves garlic, crushed

1 cup/200g piece smoked bacon or speck, diced

1/2lb/250g piece smoked ham hock or bacon bones

2 potatoes, peeled and diced

2 carrots, peeled and diced

2 turnips, peeled and diced

Stone Soup – Sopa de Pedra

2 celery stalks, diced

2 bay leaves

6 cups/1 1/2 liters vegetable or chicken stock

2 cups/500g shredded savoy or green cabbage

1 1/2 cups/400g can red kidney beans, drained
and rinsed

2 tablespoons freshly chopped
continental parsley

salt and freshly ground black pepper

Heat half the oil in a frying pan. Add sausage and cook until golden brown. Remove and set aside.

Heat remaining oil in a large saucepan over medium heat. Cook onion and garlic until soft. Add chicken stock and potatoes. **Bring** to a boil and simmer covered for 15 minutes or until tender.

Mash or puree potatoes until smooth. **Add** kale and sausage and simmer for a further 5 minutes or until kale is cooked. Season with salt and freshly ground black pepper.

Serve with crusty bread.

Green Soup – Caldo Verde

Ingredients

2 tablespoons olive oil

1 piece chourico or chorizo sausage,

peeled and sliced

1 onion, finely chopped

2 cloves garlic, crushed

7 cups/1 3/4 liters chicken stock

2.2lbs/1kg potatoes, peeled and diced

2lb/900g shredded kale or savoy cabbage

salt and freshly ground black pepper

Heat 2 tablespoons olive oil in a frying pan. Cook bread in batches until golden. Remove and drain on paper towel.

Heat remaining oil in a large saucepan over medium heat. **Cook** onion and garlic until soft.

Add chicken stock and bring to the boil. Simmer for 5 minutes. Add coriander and season with salt and pepper.

Meanwhile, fill a frying pan with 1in/2cm water and vinegar. Bring to the boil over very low heat. **Break** eggs one at a time and gently place in water. Cook until whites are just cooked. Remove with a slotted spoon.

Spoon stock in bowls and top with bread and an egg.

Bread Soup with Garlic and Eggs — Acorda à Alentejana

Ingredients

1/4 cup/60ml olive oil

6 thick slices firm bread, cut into cubes

2 onions, finely chopped

4 cloves garlic, crushed

6 cups/1 1/2 litres good chicken stock

1/4 cup/56g freshly chopped coriander (cilantro)

4 eggs, at room temperature

1 teaspoon vinegar

salt and freshly ground black pepper

Heat oil in a large saucepan over medium heat. **Add** chicken fillets and cook for 2 minutes each side or until just light golden. Add 1/2 cup/120 ml stock and simmer over low heat until chicken is cooked.

Remove and cut into thin slices. Heat remaining stock in saucepan over medium heat. Bring to the boil, add rice and cook for 12 minutes or until cooked. **Add** chicken and cook for a further 5 minutes.

Stir in lemon juice, mint and season to taste with salt and pepper.

Serve with crusty bread.

Chicken Soup with Rice, Lemon and Mint – Canja

Ingredients

1 tablespoon olive oil

1lb/500g chicken breast fillets, trimmed

8 cups/2 liters good chicken stock

3/4 cup/180ml medium or long grain rice

1/4 cup/60ml lemon juice

1/3 cup/80ml freshly chopped mint

salt and freshly ground black pepper

Heat oil in a large saucepan over medium heat. **Cook** onions, garlic and peppers until soft.

Add white wine and cook until mixture slightly reduced. **Add** tomatoes, tomato paste, stock and piri piri sauce. **Bring** to the boil and simmer for 5 minutes.

Add fish and calamari and simmer for a further 3 minutes. Add clams, cover and cook for 4-5 minutes or until clams open. Stir in coriander and season with pepper.

Spoon into bowls, remove any clams which have not opened. **Serve** with fried bread or crusty bread cut into chunks.

Ingredients

2 tablespoons olive oil

2 onions, finely chopped

3 cloves garlic, crushed

1 green peppers (capsicums),
deseeded and diced

1/2 cup/125ml white wine

4 tomatoes, diced

1/4 cup/57g tomato paste

3 cups/750ml fish stock

2-3 teaspoons piri piri sauce

1lb/400g boneless white fish fillets, cut into pieces

1/4lb/200g calamari rings

1 1/2lb/750g clams, cleaned *(see below)

1/3 cup/75g freshly chopped coriander (cilantro)

salt and freshly ground black pepper

Fisherman's Stew – Caldeirada

* *To clean clams* – place the clams
in a bowl of water and let stand for
30 minutes to free the clams from dirt.

To clean clams – place the clams in a bowl of water and let stand for 30 minutes to free clams from dirt. **Rinse** under cold running water.

Heat oil in a large saucepan over medium heat. Add garlic and cook for 1 minute.

Add mustard, white wine, stock, coriander and pepper. Bring to a boil. Add clams, cover and cook, shaking the pan from time to time, for 3-4 minutes or until clams open. **Discard** any clams that do not open.

Serve clams with wedges of lemon and crusty bread.

Ingredients

2.2lb/1kg clams, cleaned

2 tablespoons olive oil

3 cloves garlic, crushed

3 teaspoons dijon mustard

1 cup/250ml white wine

Clams Bulhao Pato – Ameijoas à Bulhão Pato

1 cup/250ml fish stock

1/4 cup/57g freshly chopped coriander (cilantro)

freshly ground black pepper

lemon wedges to serve

Place prawns in a shallow ceramic dish. **Mix** together 2 tablespoons olive oil, garlic and piri-piri sauce. Pour mixture over prawns and stir well to combine. Cover with plastic wrap and place in the fridge for 1 hour to marinate.

Heat remaining oil in a large frying pan over high heat. **Add** prawns and cook for 2-3 minutes or until prawns change color and are crisp. Remove prawns and set aside.

Pour in any remaining marinade, add white wine, stock, lemon juice, watercress and pepper. **Bring** to a boil, reduce heat to medium and cook until sauce reduces and thickens a little.

Place prawns on a serving plate, pour over sauce and serve immediately with watercress and lime wedges.

Ingredients

2.2lb/1kg medium green shrimp or prawns,

heads and shells removed leaving tails intact

1/3 cup/80ml olive oil

2 cloves garlic, crushed

1-2 teaspoons piri-piri sauce *(see below)

1/2 cup/125ml white wine

1/2 cup/125ml fish stock

Shrimp with Piri-Piri — Camaroes Piri-Piri

2 tablespoons lemon juice

2 tablespoons freshly chopped watercress

freshly ground black pepper

watercress sprigs to garnish lime wedges

*Piri Piri sauce is available from

supermarkets or specialty stores.

Heat butter in a small frying pan over medium heat. Add green onions and cook until soft. Transfer onion to a bowl and leave to cool.

Mix together mayonnaise, lemon juice, piri-piri sauce and french mustard.

Combine crab meat, eggs and parsley with green onions. Stir through mayonnaise mixture.

Spoon mixture into ramekin dishes or shells. **Sprinkle** over breadcrumbs and season with salt and pepper. Place under a hot grill and cook until breadcrumbs are golden and crisp.

Ingredients

1 tablespoon butter

6 green onions (shallots), sliced

1/2 cup/115g mayonnaise

1/4 cup/60ml lemon juice

1-2 teaspoons piri piri sauce *(see below)

2 teaspoons french mustard

1 1/2lb/700g cooked crab meat

Crab in a Cart – Santola no Carro

2 hard-boiled eggs, peeled and chopped

1 tablespoons freshly chopped
continental parsley

1 cup/230g fresh breadcrumbs

salt and freshly ground black pepper

*Piri Piri sauce is available from
supermarkets or specialty stores.

Place sardines in a large, shallow, ceramic dish. **Drizzle** with olive oil and sprinkle salt, cover with plastic and place in the fridge for 1-2 hours.

Preheat a grill or barbeque. Cook sardines for 3-4 minutes each side or until golden and cooked.

Serve with lemon wedges, boiled potatoes and salad.

For salad

Cut green and yellow pepper into four parts and remove seeds. Place on a baking tray under a hot grill for 6-8 minutes or until skin blisters. Leave to cool then remove skin and dice. **Toss** together, green pepper, tomatoes, onions, olive oil, vinegar, sugar, salt and pepper.

Grilled Sardines – Sardinhas Grelhadas

Ingredients

12 sardines, cleaned

1/4 cup/60ml extra virgin olive oil

sea salt

lemon wedges to serve

Salad

1 green pepper (capsicum), roasted

*(see below)

1 yellow pepper (capsicum), roasted

*(see below)

3 tomatoes, diced

1 red onion (spanish), diced

2 tablespoons extra virgin olive oil

1 tablespoon white wine vinegar

1/2 teaspoon sugar

salt and freshly ground black pepper

Season each fish with salt and pepper. Gently wrap 2 pieces of prosciutto around each fish and secure with toothpicks.

Heat oil and butter in a large frying pan over low to medium heat. Add trout and cook for 1-2 minutes each side or until presunto is crisp. Remove from pan.

Add garlic and cook for 1 minute. Add bay leaves, wine, stock and lemon juice. Bring to the boil and return fish to pan. Cover and simmer over low heat for 10-12 minutes or until fish is cooked. **Remove** fish from pan and discard toothpicks.

Stir through parsley. Place fish on serving plates, pour over sauce and serve with boiled potatoes and salad.

Ingredients

4 small trout, about 3/4lb/350g each,

cleaned with head and tails intact

salt and freshly ground black pepper

8 slices prosciutto

2 tablespoons olive oil

1 tablespoon butter

Trout Braganca Style – Truta à Moda de Bragança

2 cloves garlic, crushed

2 bay leaves, halved

1 cup/250ml white wine

1 cup/250ml fish stock

1/3 cup/80ml lemon juice

1 tablespoon freshly chopped continental parsley

Heat half oil in a saucepan over medium heat. Add onion and garlic and cook until soft. Add white wine, tomatoes, piri-piri paste, tomato paste and olives. **Bring** to a boil, reduce heat to low, cover and simmer for 5 minutes. Stir in lemon juice, coriander and season to taste.

Heat remaining oil in a large frying pan over medium to high heat. Season fish with salt and pepper. Cook fish for 2-3 minutes each side or until just cooked.

Serve fish with tomato sauce and fried potatoes.

Tuna Steaks in Tomato Sauce – Atum com Tomatada

Ingredients

1/3 cup/80ml olive oil

1 onion, finely chopped

2 cloves garlic, crushed

1/2 cup/125ml white wine

3 tomatoes, diced

1-2 teaspoons piri-piri sauce *(see below)

2 tablespoons tomato paste

5 tablespoons pitted black olives, sliced

1/4 cup/60ml lemon juice

1/4 cup/57g freshly chopped coriander (cilantro)

4 tuna steaks or fillets (about 1/3lb/200g each)

salt and freshly ground black pepper

*Piri Piri sauce is available in supermarkets and specialty stores.

Preheat oven to 392°F/200 °C. Lightly grease a casserole dish.

Place cod in a saucepan of water. **Bring** to a boil. Simmer over medium heat for 10-15 minutes or until fish is tender. Drain and leave to cool. **Remove** skin and bones and flake fish. If the fish is too salty, place in a bowl and cover with milk for 30 minutes. Drain and set aside.

Heat stock in a large frying pan over low heat. Add potato and simmer for 8-10 minutes or until potato is just cooked. Remove potatoes and save stock.

Heat olive oil and butter in saucepan over low to medium heat. **Add** onion and cook for 6-7 minutes or until golden.

Layer half the potatoes in the dish, top with half the cod, sprinkle with half the olives and parsley and season with pepper. Top with half the onions. Repeat again with remaining ingredients.

Combine 1/2 cup/120 ml reserved stock with lemon juice. **Pour** over potato and fish. Cover with foil and bake in the oven for 20-25 minutes. Garnish with sliced egg.

Ingredients

2.2lb/1kg boneless salt cod, soaked
*(see below)

2 cups/500ml vegetable stock

2.2lb/1kg potatoes, peeled and thinly sliced

2 tablespoons olive oil

1 tablespoon butter

3 onions, thinly sliced

24 pitted black olives

2 tablespoons freshly chopped continental parsley

1/4 cup/60ml lemon juice

2 hard-boiled eggs, peeled and sliced

Salt Cod with Potatoes and Onions –
Bacalhau à Gomes de Sa

* Soak salt cod in a bowl of cold water. Cover with
plastic wrap and place in the fridge for 24 hours,
changing the water 4 or 5 times. Drain cod, rinse well
under cold water and drain again.

Preheat oven to 428°F/220 °C

Combine 2 tablespoons olive oil, garlic, bay leaves, rosemary, paprika, cayenne pepper, salt and pepper in a mortar and pestle or small food processor. Mix or grind together to form a paste.

Coat lamb in mixture and place in a ceramic baking dish. Cover with foil and bake in the oven for 1 hour. Pour wine over meat and continue to cook for 30-40 minutes or until cooked.

Remove meat from the dish, cover and stand for 15 minutes. Pour juices into a small saucepan, draining any fat. **Add** tomato paste and cook over low heat for 3-4 minutes or until reduced a little.

Meanwhile pour remaining oil into a non-stick baking dish. **Add** potatoes and bake for 20 minutes. Add onions, carrots and peppers and bake for a further 15-20 minutes or until vegetables are golden.

Slice meat and serve with vegetables.

Lamb or Kid Roast – Cabrito Assado

Ingredients

1/3 cup/80ml olive oil

2 cloves garlic, peeled

2 bay leaves

1 tablespoon rosemary leaves

1 teaspoon ground sweet paprika

1/2 teaspoon ground cayenne pepper

salt and freshly ground black pepper

3lb/1.5kg lamb leg or kid leg

1 cup/250ml rose wine

4 potatoes, peeled and cutinto quarters

2 onions, cut into wedges

2 carrots, peeled and cut into pieces

2 red peppers (capsicum), deseeded
and cut into pieces

1 tablespoon tomato paste

Preheat oven to 400°F/200 C.

Place lamb fat side down on a board. Mix together mint, garlic, paprika, salt, pepper, olive oil and vinegar. Spread half of the mixture inside of lamb. Place prosciutto over lamb and top with red pepper. **Roll** up lamb and secure with string.

Brush lamb with remaining mixture and place on a roasting rack over a baking tray. Bake for 40-50 minutes or until cooked.

Cut lamb into slices and serve with roasted vegetables.

Lamb with Prosciutto and Mint – Carneiro à Presunto

Ingredients

1 1/2lb/750g lamb loin	2 tablespoons olive oil
1/3 cup/75g freshly chopped mint	1 tablespoon white wine vinegar
2 cloves garlic, crushed	3-4 slices presunto or prosciutto
1 teaspoon sweet paprika	1 red pepper (capsicum), roasted and sliced
salt and freshly ground black pepper	*(see below)

Preheat oven to 340°F/170 °C.

Mix together 2 tablespoons olive oil, garlic and rosemary. Brush mixture over lamb. If meat is too big for your casserole dish, roll up and secure with string.

Heat remaining oil in a large, heavy-based, flame-proof casserole dish over medium to high heat. Add meat and brown quickly on both sides. Add port and reduce by half.

Add stock, tomatoes, carrots, celery and onions. Bring to the boil. Remove from heat. Cover with foil or a lid and bake in the oven for 2 hours or until lamb is tender.

Cut meat into slices and serve with vegetables and bread.

Braised Shoulder of Lamb – Borrego Estufado

Ingredients

1/4 cup/60ml olive oil

2 cloves garlic, crushed

2 teaspoons freshly chopped rosemary

3lb/1.5kg lamb shoulder, deboned

1/2 cup/125ml port wine

1/2 cup/125ml beef stock

1 1/2 cups/400g can diced tomatoes

2 carrots, peeled and chopped

3 celery stalks, chopped

8 spring onions, trimmed

salt and freshly ground black pepper

Place liver in a shallow ceramic dish. Mix together white wine, white wine vinegar, garlic and bay leaves. **Pour** over liver. Cover with plastic wrap and place in the fridge for 1-2 hours to marinate.

Remove liver from marinade, save marinade, and pat dry with a paper towel. **Heat** 2 tablespoons oil in a large frying pan over medium to high heat. Add liver in batches and cook for 1-2 minutes each side. Remove to a plate and keep warm.

Heat remaining oil over medium heat. Cook bacon and onion until golden. Pour in marinade and cook for 5-6 minutes. Add parsley, salt and pepper. **Remove** bay leaves from sauce.

Place liver on serving plates and spoon over sauce. Serve with boiled or fried potatoes.

Liver Portuguese Style – Iscas à Portuguesea

Ingredients

1 1/2lb/750g calf's or lamb's liver, cleaned and thinly sliced

2/3 cup/160ml white wine

2 tablespoons white wine vinegar

2 tablespoons port wine

3 cloves garlic, crushed

3 bay leaves, halved

1/4 cup/60ml olive oil

3 rashers bacon, diced

1 red onion (spanish), roughly chopped

2 tablespoons freshly chopped continental parsley

salt and freshly ground black pepper

Mix together garlic, ground cumin, lemon rind, lemon juice, mustard, white wine and coriander in a shallow ceramic dish. **Add** pork and coat evenly with the mixture. Cover with plastic wrap and place in the fridge to marinate for 2-3 hours.

Heat 2 tablespoons oil in a large saucepan over medium to high heat. Remove pork from marinade with a slotted spoon, saving the marinade. Add pork and cook in batches until they turn golden. **Remove** and set aside.

Heat remaining oil over medium heat. Add onion and cook until soft. Return pork to the pan with marinade and chicken stock. Bring to the boil. **Reduce** heat to low, cover and simmer for 15-20 minutes or until pork is tender.

Season with salt and pepper and garnish with coriander leaves.

Serve pork with lemon wedges and fried potatoes.

Pork with Cumin — Rojoes à Cominho

Ingredients

3 cloves garlic, crushed

1 teaspoon ground cumin

1 lemon, rind finely grated

2 tablespoons lemon juice

2 teaspoons dijon mustard

1/2 cup/125ml white wine

1/4 cup/56g freshly chopped coriander (cilantro)

1 1/2lb/750g boneless pork, cut into 1in/2cm pieces

1/4 cup/60ml olive oil

1 onion, sliced

3/4 cup/175ml chicken stock

salt and freshly ground black pepper

coriander leaves to garnish

lemon wedges to garnish

Mix together white wine, garlic, paprika and bay leave in a shallow ceramic dish. Add pork and coat well in the mixture. Cover with plastic wrap and place in the fridge for 2-3 hours to marinate.

Heat oil in a large saucepan over medium to high heat. Remove pork from marinade with a slotted spoon, reserving marinade. **Add** pork and cook in batches until golden. Remove and set aside.

Add onion and cook until soft. Return pork to the pan with marinade, tomato paste. paprika relish and stock. Bring to the boil. **Reduce** heat to low, cover and simmer for 10-15 minutes or until pork is tender.

Add clams and toss well. Cover and cook for a further 5-10 minutes or until clams open. **Discard** any clams that are still shut.

Stir in coriander, lemon juice and pepper.

Serve with lemon wedges and bread.

Ingredients

1 cup/250ml white wine

3 cloves garlic, crushed

1 teaspoon ground sweet paprika

2 bay leaves

2 tablespoon olive oil

1 1/2lb/750g boneless pork,

cut into 1in/2cm (inches) pieces

1 onion, roughly chopped

1 tablespoon tomato paste

2 tablespoons paprika relish * (see below)

3/4 cup/175ml chicken stock

1lb/500g clams, cleaned *(see below)

1/4 cup/56g freshly chopped coriander (cilantro)

2-3 tablespoon lemon juice

Freshly ground black pepper

lemon wedges to serve

Pork with Clams Alentejo Style – Porco à Alentejana

* Paprika relish is available from specialty stores and delicatessens

* *To clean clams* – let clams stand in a bowl of water for 30 minutes to free them of dirt. Rinse under cold running water.

Mix together 2 tablespoons red wine vinegar, garlic, paprika, salt and pepper. Rub the mixture evenly over the steaks.

Heat 1 tablespoon oil in a frying pan over medium heat. Add onions and cook until golden. Add tomatoes, bay leaves and red wine. Cook for 5-10 minutes or until mixture has reduced. **Stir** through remaining red wine vinegar and parsley.

Meanwhile, in another frying pan, heat remaining oil over medium to high heat. **Add** steaks and cook for 2-3 minutes each side or until cooked to your liking.

Spoon tomato mixture over steaks and serve with chips.

Portuguese Steak with Onions – Bifes de Cebolada

Ingredients

1/4 cup/60ml red wine vinegar

2 cloves garlic, crushed

1 teaspoon ground sweet paprika

salt and freshly ground black pepper

4 medium sirloin steaks

1/4 cup/60ml olive oil

2 onions, roughly chopped

4 tomatoes, diced

2 bay leaves, halved

1/4 cup/60ml red wine

2 tablespoons freshly chopped continental parsley

Thread beef onto skewers, alternating beef cubes with onions, yellow capsicum and bay leaves. Place skewers in a shallow ceramic dish.

Mix together olive oil, red wine vinegar, garlic, parsley, salt and pepper. **Pour** over beef kebabs. Cover with plastic wrap and place in the fridge for 2-3 hours to marinate.

Cook kebabs on a barbeque grill or plate for 6-8 minutes or until cooked.

Serve kebabs with tossed salad.

Grilled Beef Kebabs – Espetada

Ingredients

4 metal skewers

1 1/4lb/650g beef fillet, cut into 1in/2cm pieces

1 red onion (spanish), cut into wedges

1 yellow pepper (capsicum)

deseeded and cut into 1in/2 cm pieces

12 fresh bay leaves

1/4 cup/60ml extra virgin olive oil

2 tablespoons red wine vinegar

3 cloves garlic, crushed

1 tablespoon freshly chopped tarragon

salt and freshly ground black pepper

Place veal in a large ceramic dish. **Mix** together olive oil, white wine vinegar, garlic, bay leaves, chillies, parsley, coriander, salt and pepper.

Pour over marinade, cover with plastic wrap and place in the fridge for 2-3 hours to marinate.

Remove veal from marinade. Cook veal on a barbeque grill or plate for 3-4 minutes on each side or until cooked, basting from time to time.

Cook onions and tomatoes on barbeque grill for 2-3 minutes on each side or until cooked.

Serve veal cutlets with onions, tomatoes and watercress.

Ingredients

4 veal cutlets

1/4 cup/60ml olive oil

1/4 cup/60ml white wine vinegar

2 tablespoons/40ml lemon juice

2 cloves garlic, crushed

2 bay leaves, crumbled

Marinated Veal Cutlets – Trouxa de Vitela

2 red chillies, deseeded and finely chopped

1 tablespoon freshly chopped continental parsley

1 tablespoon freshly chopped coriander (cilantro)

salt and freshly ground black pepper

2 red onions (spanish), cut into quarters

4 roma tomatoes, halved

1/2 bunch watercress, trimmed

Combine garlic, paprika, salt, red pepper flakes, black pepper, olive oil and lemon juice in a mortar and pestle or a small food processor. Mix together until a paste has formed.

Bash chicken pieces with a meat mallet or rolling pin to flatten slightly. With a knife, cut slits into the skin side of the chicken. Place chicken in a shallow dish. Brush marinade over the chicken. Cover with plastic wrap and place in the fridge to marinate for 2-3 hours.

Remove chicken from marinade and cook on a barbeque or grill for 30-40 minutes or until cooked, basting from time to time.

Serve chicken with salad and piri piri sauce.

Ingredients

3 cloves garlic, peeled

2 teaspoons sweet paprika

2 teaspoons coarse salt

1 tablespoon chilli flakes (medium)

Grilled Chicken – Frango Grelhado

1/4 teaspoon cracked black peppercorns

1/4 cup/60ml olive oil

1/4 cup/60ml lemon juice

3lb/1.5kg chicken, cut into 4 pieces

Preheat oven to 400°F/200 °C.

Heat oil and butter in a large, heavy-based, flame-proof casserole dish over medium to high heat. Season birds with salt and pepper. Add birds to the pan and brown all over. Remove and set aside.

Reduce heat to medium, add sausage and cook until golden and crisp. Remove and set aside.

Add onion and garlic and cook until golden. Return birds to the pan, Add cabbage, stock, wine and sausage. Bring to the boil. Remove from heat.

Cover with foil and bake in the oven for 1 hour or until birds are cooked.

Serve partridge with boiled potatoes.

Partridge with Cabbage – Perdizes com Couve

Ingredients

2 tablespoons olive oil

1 tablespoon butter

4 partridges, cleaned or

(Cornish hens or poussins)

salt and freshly ground black pepper

1/4lb/200g chourico or chorizo sausage,

peeled and sliced

2 onions, sliced

2 cloves garlic, crushed

1/2 small savoy or green cabbage,

roughly chopped

1 cup/250ml chicken stock

1/4 cup/60ml port wine

Preheat oven to 400°F/200 °C.

Heat 1 tablespoon butter in a heavy-based, flame-proof casserole dish over medium heat. **Add** onions and cook until golden.

Brush chicken all over with butter. Place chicken in casserole dish with onions, tomatoes, ham and bay leaves.

Blend together garlic, mustard, white wine, port wine, brandy, salt and pepper. Pour over chicken, cover with foil and bake in the oven for 45 minutes. **Remove** foil and baste chicken, bake for a further 20-30 minutes or until cooked and golden.

Cut chicken into pieces and serve with crispy pototoes and salad.

Jugged Chicken – Frango na Pucara

Ingredients

3 tablespoons butter

8 small onions (spring onions), peeled

3lb/1.5kg whole chicken, cleaned

3 tomatoes, cut into wedges

Less than 1/2lb or 100g smoked ham or bacon, diced

2 bay leaves

2 cloves garlic, crushed

2 teaspoons dijon mustard

1 cup/250ml white wine

1/4 cup/60ml port wine

2 tablespoons brandy

salt and freshly ground black pepper

meat and poultry

Heat 2 tablespoons oil in a large, heavy-based saucepan over medium to high heat. Add chicken in batches and cook until brown all over. Remove and set aside. Repeat with remaining chicken.

Heat remaining oil over medium heat. **Add** onions and garlic and cook until soft. Add tomatoes, carrots, yellow pepper, green pepper, bay leaves, chicken stock, tomato paste and piri-piri paste. Bring to the boil, return chicken to the pan. **Cover** and simmer over low heat for 30-40 minutes or until chicken is cooked.

Serve chicken with potatoes or rice.

Chicken Piri-Piri – Frango com Piri Piri

Ingredients

1/4 cup/60ml olive oil

4 large chicken pieces

2 onions, sliced

2 garlic cloves, crushed

1 1/2 cup/400g diced tomatoes

1 carrot, peeled and sliced

1 yellow pepper (capsicum),
deseeded and sliced

1 green pepper (capsicum),
deseeded and sliced

2 bay leaves

1 1/2 cups/375ml chicken stock

2 tablespoons tomato paste

1 tablespoon piri-piri sauce * (see below)

salt and freshly ground black pepper

*Piri Piri sauce is available from
supermarkets or specialty stores.

meat and poultry

Heat 2 tablespoons oil in a large saucepan over medium to high heat. **Add** chicken and bacon. Cook until golden. Add onion, garlic, red pepper and green pepper and cook until soft.

Add rice and stir well. Add chicken stock. Bring to a boil. **Reduce** heat to low, cover and cook for 15-20 minutes, or until rice is tender, stirring from time to time. You may need a little more stock if the rice is not tender.

Stir in olives, coriander, salt and pepper.

Serve with crusty bread.

Chicken Rice, Portuguese Style – Arroz de Galinha à Portuguesa

Ingredients

1/4 cup/60ml olive oil

1lb/500g chicken thigh fillet, diced

1/3lb/200g smoked bacon or speck, diced

1 onion, finely chopped

2 cloves garlic, crushed

1 small red pepper (capsicum), deseeded and diced

1 small green pepper (capsicum), deseeded and diced

1 1/2 cups/345g long grain rice

3 1/2 cups/875ml chicken stock

1/2 cup/115g black olives

1/3 cup/75g freshly chopped coriander (cilantro)

salt and freshly ground black pepper

Heat 2 tablespoons oil in a frying pan over medium to high heat. Add potato and cook until golden and crisp. Remove and set aside.

Heat remaining oil and butter in a saucepan over medium to high heat. Add chicken and cook until golden. Add onions and garlic and cook until soft.

Add 1 cup chicken stock, reduce heat to low and cook covered for 10 minutes or until chicken is cooked.

Mix together remaining chicken stock, egg yolks and lemon juice. Add to chicken with parsley, salt and pepper. **Stir** until mixture just comes to the boil and thickens, (mixture will curdle if it boils).

Stir through potatoes and serve with rice.

Chicken Fricassee – Galinha de Fricasse

Ingredients

4 tablespoons olive oil

2 potatoes, peeled and cut into 1/2in/1 1/2cm cubes

1 tablespoon butter

1 1/2lb/750g chicken thigh fillets, diced

1 onion, roughly chopped

2 cloves garlic, crushed

1 1/4 cups/310ml chicken stock

2 egg yolks, lightly beaten

2 tablespoons lemon juice

1 tablespoon freshly chopped continental parsley

salt and freshly ground black pepper

Preheat oven to 356°F/180 °C.

Heat oil in a large, heavy-based, flame-proof casserole dish over medium to high heat. Add rabbit in batches and cook until golden. Remove and set aside.

Add onions, garlic and presunto and cook until onions are soft. Add stock, red wine, port and bay leaves. **Bring** to the boil and return rabbit to pan.

Cover with foil and bake in the oven for approximately 1 hour or until rabbit is tender. Stir through parsley and season with salt and pepper.

Serve with potatoes and crusty bread.

Rabbit in Red Wine – Coelbo à Beira

Ingredients

1/4 cup/60ml olive oil

3lb/1.5kg rabbit, cut into small pieces

2 onions, sliced

2 cloves garlic, thinly sliced

1 presunto or prosciutto, cut into three

1 cup/250ml chicken stock

1/2 cup/125ml red wine

1/4 cup/60ml port

4 bay leaves

2 tablespoons freshly chopped continental parsley

salt and freshly ground black pepper

Preheat oven to 338°F/170 °C.

Place sugar and water in a small saucepan. Stir over low heat until sugar dissolves.

Bring to the boil, increase heat to medium-high and boil for 10-12 minutes or until mixture turns golden.

Pour mixture into 4 x 1in cup or 8 x 1/2cm cup ramekin dishes.

Whisk together eggs and sugar in a mixing bowl. Place milk and cream in a saucepan. Stir over medium heat until mixture nearly comes to the boil. Slowly whisk together milk, eggs and wine until smooth.

Pour custard into ramekins dishes. Place ramekin dishes in a large baking tray. Pour boiling water around the ramekins to fill half the baking tray. Bake in the oven for 25-35 minutes or until cooked. Time will depend on the size of the ramekin dish.

Remove from water and place in the fridge overnight to set.

Run a knife around the edge of the ramekins and turn out onto a plate to serve.

Ingredients

3/4 cup/165g caster sugar

3/4 cup/185ml water

4 eggs, at room temperature

1/3 cup/85g caster sugar, extra

1 cup/250ml milk

1 cup/250ml thickened cream

2 tablespoons port wine

Caramel Custard – Pudim Flan

Preheat oven to 400°F/200 °C. Lightly grease a 8in/20cm or 9in/22cm springform pan with butter and dust with sugar.

Place sugar and water in a heavy-based saucepan. **Stir** over low heat until sugar dissolves. Bring to the boil, increase heat a little and boil for 10-12 minutes or until thick or reaches the thread stage. **Set** aside to cool slightly.

Place egg yolks and eggs in a mixing bowl. Using electric beaters, beat eggs until light and fluffy. Gradually pour in a thin stream of sugar syrup, beating continuously. Beat in almond meal and cinnamon.

Transfer mixture to a clean saucepan and stir over low heat for 2-3 minutes until mixture thickens slightly. Do not allow to boil.

Pour mixture into prepared pan and bake in the oven for 25-30 minutes or until cooked and firm. Custard is cooked when a skewer inserted into the middle of the custard comes out clean.

Leave to cool, then run a knife around the sides of the pan before turning onto a plate. **Dust** with icing sugar. Cut into slices and serve with cream and berries.

Ingredients

1 tablespoon butter, at room temperature

1 1/2 cups/150g sugar, plus extra sugar for dusting

1/2 cup/125ml water

10 egg yolks

Heavenly Bacon – Toucinho-do-Ceu

2 eggs

2 cups/200g almond meal

1/2 teaspoon ground cinnamon

icing sugar, to dust

desserts

Preheat oven to 400°F/200 °C. Lightly grease muffin pans.

Cut pastry into 3 1/2in/9cm rounds. **Line** muffin pans with pastry and place in the fridge.

Place sugar eggs and yolks in a mixing bowl. Whisk together until well combined. Add milk, cream and vanilla essence and stir to combine.

Pour mixture into pastry cases being careful not to fill them to the top. Bake in the oven for 12-15 minutes or until golden.

Ingredients

4 sheets prepared puff pasty

1/4 cup/56g caster sugar

2 eggs

2 egg yolks

1 cup/250ml milk

1/2 cup/125ml thickened cream

1 teaspoon vanilla essence

Portuguese Custard Tarts –
Leite-Crème Portuguesa

Preheat grill to medium high.

Trim the stems of the figs, and cut 2 slits in the top of each fig. Gently open the figs. Place figs on a shallow, oven-proof dish. **Sprinkle** evenly with 2 tablespoons brown sugar. Place under grill for 4-5 minutes or until sugar melts and bubbles.

Meanwhile, place remaining sugar and wine in a small saucepan. Stir until sugar dissolves. Simmer over low heat for 3-4 minutes or until mixture thickens to a syrup-like consistancy.

Drizzle syrup over figs, sprinkle with almonds and serve with a dollop of macarpone cheese.

Figs with Port Wine – Figos com Porto

Ingredients

8 fresh figs

5 tablespoons brown sugar

1/3 cup/80ml port wine

1/4 cup/56g blanched almonds, toasted

mascarpone cheese to serve

Place milk, cream, sugar, lemon rind and cinnamon stick in a saucepan. Heat until mixture nearly comes to a boil. **Remove** from heat and discard lemon strips and cinnamon stick.

Place water and salt in a heavy-based saucepan over medium heat. Bring to a boil. Stir in rice and reduce heat to low simmer for 8-10 minutes, or until water is absorbed, stirring from time to time.

Add milk mixture, one half cup at a time, stirring from time to time until milk is absorbed. **Repeat** this until all the milk is used.

Stir in egg yolks, stirring continuously until rice is creamy, do not over cook egg yolks.

Spoon pudding into individual dishes, sprinkle with cinnamon sugar and garnish with lemon rind. Serve hot or cold.

Rice Pudding – Arroz Doce

Ingredients

2 cups/500ml milk

1 cup/250ml thickened cream

1/3 cup/75g caster sugar

1 lemon, rind cut into 3 strips

1 cinnamon stick

2 cups/500ml water

1/2 teaspoon salt

1 cup/225g medium-grain rice, (calrose)

2 egg yolks, lightly beaten

1/2 teaspoon cinnamon sugar

lemon rind to garnish

Place peaches in a large bowl. Cover with boiling water and leave for 30-60 seconds. Using a slotted spoon, remove peaches from boiling water and run under cold water.

Remove skins and transfer peaches to a bowl.

Place rose wine, sugar and cinnamon stick in a saucepan. Bring to a boil, stirring until sugar has dissolved. **Simmer** over low heat for 5 minutes.

Add peaches to syrup and cook over low heat for 5-10 minutes or until peaches are tender. Place in the fridge to cool.

Serve peaches cold with syrup.

Peaches in Red Wine — Pessago com Vinho

Ingredients

4 ripe peaches, halved and stones removed

3 cups/750ml mateus rose wine

1/2 cup/112.5g caster sugar

1 cinnamon stick

Register